One Hope

One Hope

Re-Membering the Body of Christ

Julie K. Aageson, John Borelli, John Klassen, Derek Nelson, Martha Stortz, Jessica Wrobleski

Augsburg Fortress and Liturgical Press
Minneapolis and Collegeville, Minnesota

ONE HOPE

Re-Membering the Body of Christ

Writers: Julie K. Aageson, John Borelli, John Klassen, Derek Nelson, Martha Stortz, Jessica Wrobleski

Cover design: Alisha Lofgren

Augsburg Fortress print ISBN: 978-1-4514-9652-9

Augsburg Fortress eBook ISBN: 978-1-4514-9653-6

Liturgical Press print ISBN: 978-0-8146-4812-4

Liturgical Press eBook ISBN: 978-0-8146-4837-7

The paper used in this publication meets the minimum requirements of American National Standard for Information Sciences — Permanence of Paper for Printed Library Materials, ANSI Z329.48-1984.

Manufactured in the USA

This book was produced using PressBooks.com, and PDF rendering was done by PrinceXML.

Contents

Foreword   vii

1. Re-Membering   1

What Do We Remember?   4
How Do We Re-Member?   9

2. Praying and Breathing   13

Why This Matters   15
Shared Witness   18
Shared Practices   19
Shared Hope   23

3. Eating and Drinking   25

Why This Matters   27
Shared Witness   30
Shared Practices   31
Shared Hope   34

4. Singing and Worshiping   35

Why This Matters   38
Shared Witness   40
Shared Practices   41
Shared Hope   46

5. Forgiving and Reconciling   49

    Why This Matters   51
    Shared Witness   52
    Shared Practices   55
    Shared Hope   61

6. Serving and Seeking Justice   63

    Why This Matters   65
    Shared Witness   66
    Shared Practices   69
    Shared Hope   72

7. Dying and Grieving   75

    Why This Matters   77
    Shared Witness   79
    Shared Practices   80
    Shared Hope   85

8. Bread for the Journey   87

    Discussion Questions   89

Foreword

In late summer 2014, the six authors of this book gathered at a retreat center situated in the quiet farmlands of southern Minnesota. Three Lutherans and three Roman Catholics, they responded to the invitation of Augsburg Fortress (a Lutheran publishing house) and Liturgical Press (a Catholic publishing house) to create together a resource to help Protestants and Catholics observe together the 500th anniversary of the Reformation.

These authors include:

- Ms. Julie K. Aageson (retired, ELCA [Evangelical Lutheran Church in America] Resource Centers)

- Dr. John Borelli (Georgetown University, Washington, DC)

- Abbot John Klassen (Saint John's Abbey, Collegeville, Minnesota)

- Rev. Dr. Derek Nelson (Wabash College, Crawfordsville, Indiana)

- Dr. Martha Stortz (Augsburg College, Minneapolis, Minnesota)

- Dr. Jessica Wrobleski (Wheeling Jesuit University, Wheeling, West Virginia)

Using a collaborative writing process known as Book Sprints, facilitated by its gently persistent founder, Adam Hyde, and fueled by daily prayer and seemingly endless conversation from dawn to dusk over a period of five days, these six theologians developed the resource you now have in your hands.

With *One Hope*, the authors and publishers intend to provide a tool to bring us one modest step closer to fulfillment of the hope for Lutheran-Catholic unity with the 500th anniversary of the Reformation in mind. May God bless and guide our journey forward together.

1

Re-Membering

In Tattoos on the Heart, *Father Greg Boyle, SJ, shares the story of a former gang member in Los Angeles. Jose remembers his mother telling him over and over again, "I wish you'd kill yourself; you're such a burden to me." When he was a child, she beat him to the point that he had to wear three T-shirts to school to soak up all the blood. Kids teased him: it was 100 degrees, and Jose had on three T-shirts!*

He left home as soon as he could, joining a gang in an attempt to find the family and feeling of belonging he'd never had. But like his mother's beatings, gang life marked him, too. Tattoos tagged him as being part of this family rather than that one—a family defined by common enemies. Eventually, Jose left that home as well.

Now Jose works at Homeboy Industries, the corporation Father Boyle began to stop gang violence.

Now the "wounds" the gang inflicted are gone: Jose had his tattoos removed.

Now Jose wears just one T-shirt. It says "Homeboy Industries" on the front, and on the back are the words "Nothing stops a bullet like a job."

Now Jose talks differently about the wounds his mother left: "I used to be ashamed of my wounds. I didn't want anybody to see them. Now, my wounds are my friends. I welcome my wounds. I run my fingers over my wounds. After all, how can I help the wounded, if I don't welcome my own wounds?"[1]

. . .

Like Jose's, each body could tell a history. We too are marked women and men, worshiping in marked churches. Christians have always been marked—by persecution, by their own divisions, by the times and places in which they have lived. At the first public gatherings after persecution ended, Christian leaders showed up with the marks of torture on their bodies.

The risen Christ showed up with marks of torture on his body, too. The apostle Thomas insists on welcoming Jesus' wounds: "Unless I see the mark of the nails in his hands, and put my finger in the mark of the nails, and my hand in his side, I will not believe" (John 20:25). Christ obliges, opening his body for Thomas to touch his wounds (v. 27). Only in touching does Thomas know that the body in front of him belongs to the risen Christ.

---

1. Gregory Boyle, *Tattoos on the Heart: The Power of Boundless Compassion* (New York: Free Press, 2010).

The church is the body of Christ in the world today, and it too bears marks of persecution and violence. Our communions, Lutheran and Catholic, are wounded by five hundred years of division. Furthermore, we live on a marked planet, wounded by violence, ethnic struggle, ecological destruction, inequality, and grinding poverty.

How do we deal with our wounds?

As a group of Lutheran and Catholic authors, we face this question, not with an answer, but with gestures of resistance: we wish to *re-member*—bone on bone and flesh on flesh—the broken body of Christ. We remember as we recall a divided history, and we remember in our longing for a common future. Just like the body of the risen Christ, the church bears wounds—a "double-woundedness" that has been officially acknowledged by both Lutheran and Catholic leaders. Yet despite our division and because of those wounds, the church is the body that people long to touch as Thomas did.

The earliest theologians spoke of the marks of the church: one, holy, catholic, and apostolic. We may not yet be fully one; our unholiness is often apparent in the scandals that continue to shake us; we struggle to be catholic, that is, inclusive and universal; and our theologians argue over very different understandings of apostolicity. But our two communions agree that we witness to that marked body of Christ in the world through the practices we share. In these gestures of resistance, we remember who and whose we are. And we trust that God will re-member us, bringing us together in new ways for the life of the world.

One Hope

Out of these broken pieces, these wounded members, God promises a new creation.

What Do We Remember?

The year 2017 represents a remarkable anniversary—one that all Christians should know something about, because it makes us who we are today. Five hundred years earlier, on October 31, 1517, a German monk named Martin Luther (1483–1546) sent shock waves through Europe when he sent a letter called "Disputation on the Efficacy and Power of Indulgences" (better known as the Ninety-Five Theses) to the archbishop of Mainz and the bishop of Brandenburg. Luther had no intention of causing a break among Christians. Rather, he wanted an open discussion on an issue that truly troubled him—the widespread Christian practice called indulgences.

Luther believed that the pursuit of indulgences was misguided. He insisted that it distorted Christian spirituality, because it led Christians to misunderstand sin and forgiveness. An indulgence is a remission of temporal *punishment* for sins whose *guilt* has already been forgiven. An analogy might be a mother who forgives her child for breaking curfew but still insists on the punishment of grounding the child for two weeks. An indulgence would remove even that punishment. Luther felt that seeking an indulgence obscured a central aspect of the faith, making human effort to escape punishment the center, rather than God's initiative in offering forgiveness.

Efforts over the past fifty years at resolving this major theological issue have been encouraging and unifying. Lutherans and Roman Catholics have shared with each other how each side thinks about forgiveness and God's grace. The historic 1999 Lutheran-Catholic *Joint Declaration on the Doctrine of Justification* put the matter this way: it is "by grace alone, in faith in Christ's saving work and not because of any merit on our part, we are accepted by God and receive the Holy Spirit, who renews our hearts while equipping and calling us to good works."[2]

So two faith communities are closer on theology today. But the division was never just theological. In fact, a whole array of political, social, and ecclesiastical interests converged on the trajectory for reform that Martin Luther inaugurated. These forces took on a robust life of their own, beyond the control of even the most powerful princes of the time. By 1530 a break seemed final, despite the best intentions for unity by Lutheran reformers and the pope's and emperor's theologians. (Luther's ruler, Emperor Charles V, had sided with the papacy.) The 1530 *Augsburg Confession* outlined the Lutheran version of the faith. It was refuted by the Roman Catholic *Confutation*. Both sides agreed on core doctrines of the Trinity, the incarnation of Christ, and baptism. But Lutheran teachings on the church and sacraments could not be reconciled with the Roman Catholic ones.

In a climate that emphasized force and ultimatum, meager efforts at dialogue failed. Finally, by 1545, when the reform

---

2. Lutheran World Federation and Roman Catholic Church, *Joint Declaration on the Doctrine of Justification* (Grand Rapids, MI: Eerdmans, 2000), par. 15.

Council of Trent was convoked, the split was real and irreversible. Catholics might say that the Protestant Reformation had gone too far by then to turn back. Lutherans might say that the response from Rome had been so inadequate for so long that they needed to go their own way.

As the two church bodies went their separate ways, each remembered what had happened differently. Facts are facts, but they can be strung together into very different stories. In the hundred-year anniversaries that followed 1517, Protestants used this anniversary to promote their differences with Catholics. In 1617, they used the commemoration to stabilize and revitalize a common Protestant identity for Lutherans and Reformed (Calvinist) Christians, defined by their shared differences from Catholicism. In 1717, Protestants minted coins depicting the posting of the theses on the Wittenberg castle church door. The 1817 anniversary came close on the heels of a Prussian-led defeat of Napoleon, and Prussia used the occasion to lay a foundation stone for a monument in Wittenberg's plaza. Luther was made an emblem for Prussian unity and superiority. In 1917, German leaders rallied their people by portraying Luther as a national hero amidst the terrible losses of World War I. But in 2017, Protestants and Catholics have an opportunity to commemorate the events of 1517 differently.

Lutherans and Catholics have engaged in church-sponsored dialogues for fifty years. Meanwhile, their officials have promoted common prayer, joint Scripture study, cooperative efforts in social action, and other shared activities.

As a result, they now have a real opportunity to emphasize together their unity for the good of all and for the whole world. The turning point came at Vatican II, the gathering of the world's Catholic bishops that happened between 1962 and 1965. There an overwhelming number of bishops voted, in the presence of Lutheran and other Protestant observers, to base future ecumenical engagement on the recognition that these other Christians take Scripture and creedal dogma as normative. Their churches administer the sacramental means of saving grace. The time was ripe for a sincere dialogue in truth and charity. After numerous agreed statements and a growing consensus on several essential aspects of faith, the singular achievement of a signed agreement on the doctrine of justification by faith came in 1999. The dialogue continued into the new millennium, and in 2013, the Commission on Unity offered a lengthy report preparing for the 2017 commemoration on the theme of "From Conflict to Communion."

Above all, the report insists, in whatever they undertake together, Catholics and Lutherans should always begin from the greater unity they share and not from the remaining (but often more noticeable) differences that divide them. Emphasizing their greater unity strengthens the joy flowing from what they hold in common. That report also insists that Lutherans and Catholics should surrender to the ongoing transformation of their encounters by their mutual witness. In such a way, Catholics and Lutherans will renew their commitments to praying and undertaking efforts for visible unity and thereby rediscover the power of the gospel of Jesus Christ in their lives right now.

Lutherans and Catholics can strengthen their common witness to the mercy of God in proclamation of the good news and in service to the world. They might also imagine how what they do together in 2017 will be remembered in 2117.

Lutherans and Catholics agree that unity is God's gift to the church and not the result of any human effort. Still, they feel they must do all they can to remain in unity so they can serve the world together. The Gospel of John records this prayer of Jesus for his followers given before his passion and death: "I ask not only on behalf of these, but also on behalf of those who will believe in me through their word, that they may all be one. As you, Father, are in me and I am in you, may they also be in us, so that the world may believe that you have sent me" (John 17:20-21). The course of the growing consensus over the past fifty years to fulfill the prayer of Jesus did not follow any predicted path. Catholics and Lutherans were surprised that on justification by faith and a subsequent agreement on what makes the church apostolic, they could arrive at a sufficient but "differentiated" consensus. On the fundamental doctrines that make them Christians, Lutherans and Catholics could agree. Real and essential differences remain but do not obstruct agreement on the fundamentals of faith.

Lutherans and Catholics agree that the church is the body of Christ, that there is only one Christ, that there is only one body, and that through baptism, all become members of this body. In the words of the Commission on Unity, "In remembering with each other the beginning of the Reformation, they are taking their baptism seriously."[3] But there is much more to this commemoration. Catholics and Lutherans agree that they are called to share the healing and reconciling presence of Christ through the proclamation of his message through word and sacrament and through service to all. To remember that imperative is to begin to welcome our wounds as Christians living in division.

How Do We Re-Member?

Sometimes individual memories come to us unbidden. But usually the task of memory is real work. Toward the end of his *Confessions*, Augustine reflects on the nature and significance of memory. He describes its "fields and spacious halls . . . where are stored as treasures the countless images that have been brought into them" by our experiences. "When I go into this storehouse," Augustine explains, "I ask that what I want should be brought forth. Some things appear immediately, but others require to be searched for longer and then dragged out" (X.viii).

This image of the "great hall of memory"—like a huge library with thousands of individual books stashed away—probably resonates with many people's experience. We try to recall the details of an event or a name that has been "misplaced" among countless other thoughts and experiences. Augustine's

3. Lutheran–Roman Catholic Commission on Unity, *From Conflict to Communion: Lutheran–Catholic Common Commemoration of the Reformation in 2017* (Leipzig, Germany: Evangelische Verlagsanstalt, 2013), par. 221.

description of memories as treasures in a field evokes Jesus' parable of the kingdom of heaven in Matthew 13, prompting us to contemplate how memory is significant to the task of witnessing to the peace of Christ in a broken world.

Augustine's image is appealing and evocative. But recent research on the science of memory suggests that remembering is not merely a task of retrieval; it is also a process of reconstruction. In *Pieces of Light: How the New Science of Memory Illuminates the Stories We Tell about Our Pasts,* psychologist Charles Fernyhough explains that viewing memories as physical things is misleading: "Memories are not possessions that you either have or do not have. They are mental constructions, created in the present moment, according to the demands of the present moment."[4]

For this reason, a memory is not a static thing, like an heirloom we take out of the closet on holidays. Instead, "a memory is more like a *habit*, a process of constructing something from its parts, in similar but subtly changing ways each time."[5] The fragmentary threads that our memories weave and reweave are located in our bodies and in the stories and practices that communities of people have shared over time. Often what triggers the process of recollection is a familiar smell, taste, or song, the feeling of standing in a place where we've stood before, or a friend or family member's "Remember when?"

4. Charles Fernyhough, *Pieces of Light: How the New Science of Memory Illuminates the Stories We Tell about Our Pasts* (New York: Harper Perennial, 2012), 5.
5. Ibid., 6.

The memories elicited by these sensory triggers may be random, inconsequential, or even unwanted, but as human persons and communities, we also have more deliberate ways of remembering and ritualizing the things most important to us. We acknowledge birthdays and anniversaries with candles, cake, or flowers. We mark the birth of nations as well as the terrors that have befallen them through symbol and ceremony, with the imperative that we "never forget!" Nations build monuments, fans wear team colors, and some even mark their bodies with tattoos in an attempt to preserve a sense of identity and belonging.

In a similar way, as Christians, we remember who we are not simply through looking backward and recalling what has happened in the past, but also through continuing to share and embody the gifts and practices that have made us. Musicians and athletes practice specific movements and patterns over and over again. They do so precisely in order to shape the intuitive memory of their bodies. In much the same way, the practices that bring wholeness and unity have to be made incarnate in the body of Christ, the church.

There is, moreover, an *ethical* dimension to how we remember. We need to be attentive to the facts as we understand them, first of all. But then there is the matter of motive—do we remember truly, or do we bend our recollections to serve our own interests? And we need to remain aware of the ways we employ memory in the present to unite or divide, to bring healing, restoration, and wholeness or to dwell on the wrongs of the past.

Beyond the recollection of our history in its moments of both division and reconciliation, we, the authors of this resource, wish to remember who we are as Lutherans and Catholics through several shared and ongoing embodied, human practices. We consider here praying and breathing, eating and drinking, singing and worshiping, forgiving and reconciling, serving and seeking justice, and dying and grieving. As we look forward to the next fifty, or perhaps five hundred, years of dialogue and communion, such practices will be essential to the ongoing *re-membering* and *re-forming of the body*—not just to recall our history in a commemorative and retrospective way, but also to take the broken pieces and put them back together as a new creation. Paul writes, "For not only the creation but we ourselves groan inwardly as we wait for our adoption as sons and daughters, the redemption of our bodies. For in this hope we were saved" (Rom. 8:23-24).

Our hope in writing this book is that attention to the embodied and communal practices we describe in the following chapters might help us—not only as Lutheran and Catholic Christians, but also as a human family—to truly re-member who and whose we are as we seek the healing of our wounded world. The chapters that follow are not intended to be an exhaustive or comprehensive treatment of the practices of Christian life, but are rather a shared meditation on the ways that we may not only welcome the wounds that mark us, but also begin to heal them.

2

Praying and Breathing

"I don't know what to pray for," the woman acknowledged as she watched the monitors beeping around her. Her husband lay gravely ill, afflicted with a terminal cancer. The immediate problem, however, was a fever, something easily treatable by massive doses of antibiotics. Should those be given, only to allow him to die of the cancer that was eating his brain? Burdened by the weight of the situation, she sat down heavily in a chair—and just breathed. Gradually, the words came: "Behold and bless. Behold and bless. Behold and bless." It calmed her, calmed the room, even—did she imagine it?—calmed the monitors.

Watching as the plane ripped into the second World Trade Center tower even as the first still burned, the college president phoned his closest advisers and campus ministry team. "I don't know what's happening in downtown Manhattan," he said. "But gather the community in the chapel at noon for a prayer service."

The older brother phoned his siblings. "We finally found a good place for mom," he announced. "It's an answer to prayer." As their

13

mother's Alzheimer's progressed, it had become increasingly clear that she could no longer live at home. They had begun looking, only to find facilities for memory care with long waiting lists. The family had redoubled its efforts; they also prayed and asked for prayers from friends, priests, and pastors. Did the cumulative power of prayer "work"? Or was their success the fruit of their concerted effort? And in the end, did it matter?

. . .

These three vignettes of prayer illustrate some of the many forms prayer can take: individual and communal, words and silence, intercession and thanksgiving. All prayer, all human yearning, is fundamentally a response to God's initial prayer over the face of the waters in the first chapter of Genesis. With God's prayer—God's breath—life came into being. That same spirit of God animated the first human. Human birth reenacts this first prayer as doctors, midwives, or parents watch for a child's first breath, which seems to come from nowhere. In fact, that first breath does come from somewhere—or, more accurately, from Someone—the One who breathed us and prayed us into being in the first place.

How do we respond to that first prayer, God's breath in us, God's breath enlivening us? It's easy: breathe in, breathe out; inhale, exhale. Breathe in Spirit; breathe out blessing. Breathing connects us with our animating Spirit; it's always enough. Worship leaders who know this create space after giving the invitation, "Let us pray." Then they pause. But really, they take a breath, making an opening to breathe in the Spirit of God, who breathed everything into being. Not a bad move.

Why This Matters

We first encounter God as Spirit, the breath that gives us life, just as Job acknowledged that "the spirit of God has made me, and the breath of the Almighty has given me life" (Job 33:4). In certain moments when words fail, when we do not know what to pray for or what to say, we can pray by simply acknowledging the breath that gives us life. We can count on the Spirit to pray for us, "for we do not know how to pray as we ought, but that very Spirit intercedes with sighs too deep for words" (Rom. 8:26). At an interreligious service in Assisi in 1986, involving leaders of dozens of religions and Christian communions, Pope John Paul II echoed the apostle Paul: "We can indeed maintain that every authentic prayer is called forth by the Holy Spirit, who is mysteriously present in the heart of every person."

Sometimes, though, we humans need words to accompany the mysterious work of the Spirit. Sometimes we want to respond to God not only with breath, but also with speech. Prayer speaks, responding to God's invitation to conversation. Prayer talks back to God in direct address. All the really important encounters in Scripture require quotation marks.

Three of the most important words in the Bible are "then God said." We should pay attention whenever we hear these words! Much of Scripture falls into third-person narration:

they went here; *they* went there; *they* talked about this and that. When the "this and that" they talked about is meant to really grip us, it's often in direct speech, the words in red letters.

Prayer inserts us into the ongoing conversation between Creator and creatures. Who wouldn't want to be in on *that* conversation? The question is: how to join in?

A Jesuit friend describes his own journey of joining in. Listen to the cadence of talking and listening in his prayer: "First, I talked at God the way you'd talk at someone sitting next to you on a plane. Then I talked to God as someone I was beginning to know. At some point, I found myself talking with God as with a trusted friend. Then I listened to God, since God seemed to be talking back. Now mostly I listen for God, sometimes into the silence, trusting that someone is there." This man acknowledges a common experience in personal prayer: a lot of times, nothing happens. "But," he went on, "you'd hate not to be there on the day that something did."

Throughout the centuries, Christians have struggled with what to say in prayer. After watching Jesus wander off to pray and marking his absence in terms of days, rather than hours, the disciples demanded, "Teach us to pray!" (Luke 11:1). Jesus responded by teaching them the Lord's Prayer, which follows a classical Jewish form of prayer: naming God, praising God, asking God for what we need. The radical element in Jesus' prayer was to address God as "Abba" (we would say "Papa" or "Daddy" in English). It was an intimate way of addressing the author of the universe. No one had prayed in this way before.

Worship is communal prayer, blending the voices of the people together as one. Calling and responding to each other and to God, we imitate the call and response that is at the heart of prayer. Coming together as a community for prayer also provides the support, affirmation, and witness of many brothers and sisters. It's powerful. One worshiper may not know exactly what to say to God in prayer, but the next person in the pew might give it words. The words could even come from the past. There is power in joining one's voice to prayers spoken across centuries and around the world.

The psalms are the quintessential form of communal prayer. Our two communions share—along with all Christians, as well as our Jewish brothers and sisters—the Psalter, the collection of 150 psalms that make up the book of Psalms. The psalms are direct communication with God, punctuated by phrases to get God's attention: "Lord, hear my prayer; listen to my cry for mercy" (143:1), "Hear my cry, O Lord; listen to my prayer" (61:1), "Hear my prayer, Lord; listen to my cries for help" (39:12). There is urgency in these phrases: "Listen up!" "Hey, you!" The psalms aim to get God's attention. And the psalmist sang the blues, too: many of the psalms are laments. Other psalms are poignant pleas for forgiveness. The psalms are full of rejoicing and praising God. Finally, psalms of intercession ask for what we need. The whole array of human emotions and longings is given voice, and the voice speaks both to God and from God.

Jesus encourages his disciples in biblical times and in our own time to ask for what they need (Matt. 7:7; Luke 11:9). We don't always know what we need, and we don't always get what we ask for. Nevertheless, intercessory prayer puts us in a posture of dependence on the God who breathes us into life.

Shared Witness

Not surprisingly, prayer also gives life to the ecumenical movement. The New Testament urges us to maintain the unity of the Spirit: "There is one body and one Spirit, just as you were called to the one hope of your calling, one Lord, one faith, one baptism, one God and Father of all, who is above all and through all and in all" (Eph. 4:3-6). If we take this passage to be a statement about Christian life today, it is a statement that can only be made in faith. Sometimes the unity of the one body can be very difficult to discern.

The Vatican II *Decree on Ecumenism* regards individual and communal prayer for the unity of Christians as the heart of the ecumenical movement. It states forthrightly, "There can be no ecumenism worthy of the name without interior conversion. . . . This change of heart and holiness of life, along with public and private prayer for the unity of Christians, should be regarded as the soul of the whole ecumenical movement, and merits the name, 'spiritual ecumenism.'"[1] No one lacks the qualifications for spiritual ecumenism. It begins with prayer, which is part of the everyday lives of Christians.

---

1. Second Vatican Council, Decree on Ecumenism (*Unitatis Redintegratio*), November 21, 1964, pars. 7–8, in *Vatican Council II: The Conciliar and Postconciliar Documents*, ed. Austin Flannery, new revised edition (Collegeville, MN: Liturgical Press, 2014).

John Paul II firmly placed ecumenism at the center of the church's work, giving priority to prayer as a way of achieving greater unity. Likewise, the Lutheran World Federation declares, "To be Lutheran is to be ecumenical. We are committed to the quest for visible unity of the Church. . . . For us, Christian ecumenism is not a choice: it is our mission to witness together with and in Christ, and it is a gift we receive from God through the Holy Spirit."[2] The question, then, is not *whether* to pray with and for each other, but *how.*

Shared Practices

At the most basic level, Lutherans and Catholics can help one another pray. They can pray together, in long stretches of silent meditation or in communal prayers. For centuries, Christians have practiced rich forms of meditation and prayer, which include the following.

Breathing

Happily, breathing is a practice we don't have to *work* at, but as Christians, we need to *think* about breathing. We breathe in the life-giving Spirit that first gave us life; we breathe out blessing. Centering prayer follows and focuses on breath or a word until we are unaware of distractions.

---

2. Lutheran World Federation, "Ecumenical Relations," www.lutheranworld.org /content/ecumenical-relations.

Attentive Reading of Scripture

Protestants and Catholics share a common book: the Bible. We read Scripture to learn about God and God's people, and also for insight, wisdom, and guidance. Most important, we read Scripture to encounter the Spirit who gives us life. Scripture has always served as a prod to prayer. Over time, a practice of prayerful reading, called "divine reading" or *lectio divina*, evolved in many communities. *Lectio* aims not so much at *broad* reading, but at *deep* reading. It is a loose format in which short biblical passages are read slowly and "chewed on" in silent reflection and prayer, individually or in community.

The *Examen*

Ignatius of Loyola (1491–1556), the founder of the Jesuits, developed a practice of prayer that saw daily life as a kind of text for reflection. He commended the practice to people at midday, but particularly at day's end. The *examen* involves taking time to seek the guidance of the Spirit in order to quietly review the events of the day and one's responses to them. One pays particular attention to one's failings, as well as to reasons for gratitude. The prayer can be done individually or with a partner or spouse; the important thing is learning to see one's life with the grateful, loving, and merciful eyes of Jesus. One couple prayed the *examen* every night, pausing particularly to remember together what they were thankful for. When the husband was diagnosed with a catastrophic and fatal illness, they continued the practice, pausing every night to be grateful. After he died, his wife reported, "There was never a night where we said, 'The best thing about today is that it's over!' There was always something to give thanks for."

Repetitive Prayer

Another form of prayer involves repetition of a phrase so that it might become a prayer of the heart. Some people use the "Hail Mary"; others repeat the Jesus Prayer, "Lord Jesus Christ, Son of God, have mercy on me, a sinner"; still others hold fast to an ancient Orthodox prayer, the Trisagion: "Holy God, Holy and Mighty, Holy and Immortal, have mercy on us." Luther reportedly wrestled down the devil by repeating over and over again a prayer his religious superior gave him: "I am yours, save me." Whatever the words, these prayers tune the one who prays to the melodies of grace.

Communal Prayer

Communal prayer was one of the features of the apostolic church (see Acts 2:42). The prayers recited in common include the Our Father—the prayer Jesus taught his disciples—and the psalms. The psalms were treasured as prayers in the early church communities from the beginning, since many of the first Christians continued following their Jewish forms of prayer. Prayer in common continues into the present, despite divisions among Christians. The revised *Ecumenical Directory* of the Catholic Church recommends that "shared prayer is in itself a way to spiritual reconciliation" and "prayer in common is recommended for Catholics and other Christians so that together they may put before God the needs and problems they share—for example, peace, social concerns, mutual charity among people, the dignity of the family, the effects of poverty, hunger and violence, and others."[3]

Common Celebration

A tradition of Lutherans and Catholics celebrating milestones along the way of their ecumenical journey has emerged. In 1980, there were special services celebrating the 450th anniversary of the Augsburg Confession and a Lutheran-Catholic joint statement for that occasion, *All under One Christ*. Similar events in 1983 surrounded the 500th anniversary of Martin Luther's birth and the joint statement *Martin Luther—Witness to Christ*. Officials from the Vatican and the Lutheran World Federation led services of prayer and thanksgiving to mark the signing of the *Joint Declaration on the Doctrine of Justification* in Augsburg in 1999. Catholics and Lutherans should convene services to inspire prayer, attention to Scripture, joint action, and mutual witness in the years ahead, thinking ecumenically about the last five hundred years of their shared journey.

---

3. Pontifical Council for Promoting Christian Unity, *Directory for the Application of Principles and Norms on Ecumenism*, March 25, 1993, pars. 108–9.

Shared Hope

As we engage in these practices, individual and communal, we pray with Christians across the centuries and around the world, regardless of their communions. We pray with anyone who prays in the Spirit, and our prayers have power, as Jesus assures his disciples (Matt. 7:7). To pray with someone is to let go of control, to open oneself to the possibilities that only God can supply. Our thoughts follow their own course, leading, we pray in faith, somewhere closer to God.

A colleague from the civil rights movement in the American South remembers the impact of prayer: "When they prayed the Lord's Prayer, white people had to acknowledge they were praying the same prayer as black people in the shanty churches on the other side of the tracks. They prayed the same prayer—and they prayed to the same Father." Over time, the spirit of that prayer eroded their racism. Prayer is like that, calling all of us to deeper awareness of the way that God's Spirit is as near to us as our own breath, continually at work in our lives and in the world around us.

3

Eating and Drinking

A queue of hungry people three deep winds its way around the dining area and out into the entrance of the community's homeless shelter. Waiting restlessly are families with young children, teenagers, women and men whose faces reflect the unfairness of life, even a familiar neighbor fallen on hard times—all of them hungry and eager for the evening's feast. Those who prepared the meal wonder: Will there be enough food? Will it satisfy? Is it good enough? They join with the diners in offering thanks, celebrating the anticipation of the meal to come.

The food is served. There are exchanges of thanks and appreciation from the servers as well as the served, comments about the day's events, complaints about the weather. In all of this, the food conveys the elemental stamp of common need, common hunger, and the importance of feeding one another.

. . .

Food and drink have to do with our deepest needs and the deepest needs of the world. Whether we are Catholics, Lutherans, agnostics, or ones who no longer find the life of the church nourishing, we all understand the delight, necessity, and privilege of eating and drinking. *In the act of eating and drinking, we are all literally re-membered—made whole, filled, restored.* The absence of hunger in a person is usually a bad sign. Not everyone is hungry for a sacramental kind of eating, but for Catholics and Lutherans at least, sacramental life is central to our understanding of being part of the body of Christ. A sacrament is a tangible, physical expression of God's grace. We agree that in the sacrament of Holy Communion, Christ is present. We believe that Christ's sacrifice on the cross brings forgiveness and restoration to new life. We eat and drink each week at the table of the Lord—"the body of Christ, broken for you; the blood of Christ, shed for you," to which we respond, "Amen."

In the film *Babette's Feast* (1987, Criterion Collection), a French chef offers her culinary gifts to an isolated community off the coast of Denmark. To people who have eaten only fish broth and coarse bread all their lives, Babette serves a feast unlike any they have ever seen, much less tasted. In the pleasure of the food and the company around the table, and because of Babette's generosity, old grudges are buried, rifts are mended, forgiveness is offered, and love is shared. It is a picture, however inadequate, of how the rituals of eating and drinking become sacramental. They are essential for our growth as children of God.

You don't have to be a chef like Babette to find deep pleasure in planning a dinner, carefully choosing favorite recipes, preparing a beautiful table, and serving the finest food you can offer to friends and family. But it isn't just the food that draws us to the table again and again. It is the larger sense of what the table signifies: hospitality and welcome. The conversations that ensue also nourish the people gathered. What we find at the table is life-giving, not just as food and drink, but as communion.

Communion involves *exchange*. Potatoes and a roast might be passed between people who eat together, but so are events of the day, emotions, and memories: the stuff of life. Our daily habit of eating, whether alone or with others, is a reminder of our dependence on food, drink, and the generosity of a God who promises to come to us in bread and wine. The sacramental life of the church points to the deeper meanings of food and drink, and invites us into its mysteries.

Why This Matters

Eating and drinking connect us to the earth and sustain our bodies. Gathering together to eat and drink gives us a way to welcome guests. It ties us together and makes us strong. In every culture and tradition, food and drink are a way of communing. The dinner table is where most people learn manners and ways to be respectful of others. We learn about our bodies there—sitting up straight and learning to control our hands and mouths. We learn what we like and what we don't, about what tastes good and what we would rather pass by. Sharing meals is an elemental part of human life.

In the early church, the Eucharist probably felt more like a meal in someone's home than it did a formal ritual. The presider seamlessly moved from telling a story about Jesus, to returning thanks for the gifts of food set before those gathered, to the distribution of the bread and wine. Bread baked in primitive ovens at low temperatures was unlikely to last long. ("Give us this day our daily bread"—because yesterday's is moldy.) Yet wine would last for a long time. So a simple meal of those two particular elements reinforced both the fragility and stability of life before God.

Author and activist Sara Miles writes about her experience of coming to faith in a book called *Take This Bread: A Radical Conversion*. A self-described blue-state, secular intellectual and skeptic, she tells about the first time she entered a church. She was forty-six, indifferent to religion for the most part, and often dismayed by American fundamentalism. She ate a piece of bread and took a sip of wine. It was her first Communion, and as she says, it changed everything:

> Eating Jesus, as I did that day to my great astonishment, led me against all my expectations to a faith I'd scorned and work I'd never imagined. The mysterious sacrament turned out to be not a symbolic wafer at all, but actual food—indeed, the bread of life. In that shocking moment of communion, filled with a deep desire to reach for and become part of a body, I realized what I'd been doing with my life all along was what I was meant to do: feed people."[1]

---

1. Sara Miles, *Take This Bread: A Radical Conversion* (New York: Ballantine, 2007).

Miles began a kind of pilgrimage with her newly found parish, establishing a food pantry, helping in the housing projects, and learning together about the politics of food and the complications of hunger:

> I was, as the prophet said, hungering and thirsting for righteousness. I found it at the eternal and material core of Christianity: body, blood, bread, wine poured out freely, shared by all. I discovered a religion rooted in the most ordinary yet subversive practice: a dinner table where everyone is welcome, where the poor, the despised and the outcasts are honored.[2]

In eating and drinking at the table of the Lord, Christians experience the risen Christ, the bread of life. He is bread for a starved and dis-membered world. The Gospel of Luke tells us that after Jesus had been crucified and raised from the dead, he "came near" to two of his disciples while they were on the road to the village of Emmaus, yet they failed to recognize him. It was only when he took bread, breaking it and giving it to them, that "their eyes were opened, and they recognized him" (24:13-35). Similarly, it is in *our* experience of broken bread that *our* eyes are opened to Christ who is really present in our lives, transforming us and, through us, our world. We begin to see as Christ sees, which means we notice that others hunger. Others need us. Feeding other people is, as Miles says, at the "eternal and material core of Christianity." Being nourished by God's presence in the Eucharist, we cannot help but be awakened to the hungers of the people around us, in whom Christ is also present.

2. Ibid.

The kernels of grain brought by a family were given to a group of children in the parish, who ground the kernels into flour, added water, and kneaded it to form loaves that, when baked, filled the church with mouth-watering fragrance and became First Communion bread. Like the boy who shared his lunch at Galilee (John 6:5-13), our small offerings are multiplied in Jesus' hands, and we are empowered to share this abundance with others. Our eyes are opened to the goodness of the earth itself, which brings forth fruit in its season to sustain us.

In the Liturgy of the Eucharist, the presider prays, "*Blessed are you, Lord God of all creation, for through your goodness we have received the bread we offer you: fruit of the earth and work of human hands, it will become for us the bread of life.*" In the acts of eating and drinking, we are the recipients of God's good earth, caring for our own bodies together with all the other bodies of the world so that we might become the body of Christ, whole and holy.

Shared Witness

In the sacramental life of the church, we celebrate eating and drinking so that Christ might live in us. It's a mystery, this fundamental necessity of bread and wine, food and drink conveying God, bearing Christ, filling us and sending us into the world as Christ's body. The gifts of the earth—soil, water, seeds, sun—are conduits of a loving God, basic elements for health. They are holy things, intended for all God's creation. From these holy things, we are fed and nourished and sent to be food and drink for all. In the daily agony of news from around the world about hunger, want, injustice, and fear, we share a mandate to pay attention: to feed the hungry, to make a place for the outsider, to build up, to bear Christ, to *be* Christ in a world deeply divided, broken, and hungry. God is an indiscriminate host. We should be, too.

In 1978, the Joint Lutheran–Roman Catholic Commission reached remarkable consensus in its report "The Eucharist." Despite the stretching advances toward a common understanding of the meaning of Eucharist, agreement on the sacrifice of the Eucharist, and a heritage of common Eucharistic prayers, we are not at the point of full communion. This causes great frustration and pain. Imagine a dinner party where ten guests are present but only nine are fed. Being honest about the pain of such division is perhaps one of the most powerful engines available to move our churches closer together.

Shared Practices

We hope God will do the work we have as yet been unable to accomplish. After all, God shows up in places we don't expect. Here are some places we can show up. We live into this practice by remembering in our daily eating and drinking those simple imperatives in the Eucharistic prayers we share: "Bless . . . , Break . . . , Take and eat."

Bless

Eucharist is an act of thanks to and praise of God for all good things, especially as they have come to us through the saving work of Jesus Christ. Praise and blessing are expressed at the Preparation of Gifts, in the Preface, and throughout the Eucharistic Prayer, concluding in the doxology: "Through him and with him and in him. . . ." As Christians, we carry this stance, this attitude of blessing, into every part of our lives: to our homes, tables, and offices, to our fields and laboratories, into all the activities of human living.

Break

One area of intense discussion and dialogue between our two communions is the sacrificial dimension of Eucharist. We have come to a solemn, fulsome agreement that Eucharist is a "sacrifice of praise," which is possible only because of the sacrifice of Christ on the cross, who died for us and all creation, once for all.

In celebrating Eucharist, we remember the violence of the sacrifice of Jesus on the cross and the bread that is broken as the body of Christ was once broken for us. It is good for all of us to remember the violence that is inherent in daily eating. As environmentalist William Ralph Inge notes in Michael Pollan's *The Omnivore's Dilemma*, the whole natural world functions by eating and being eaten.[3] Eat or be eaten is a basic law of nature. As we eat our daily food, we remember that

3. Michael Pollan, *The Omnivore's Dilemma* (New York: Penguin, 2006).

our lives depend on the lives of other creatures on this earth that daily give their lives for us.

Take and Eat

"Let us break bread *together*": the hymn is so familiar, we forget its radical thrust. How often do we eat together in this fast-food, eat-on-the-fly culture? When we gather around any table to eat together with others, we echo the solidarity of a Eucharistic meal. And look at the others we eat with! These are dining companions we might not necessarily choose.

The Eucharist re-members Jesus' own countercultural dining habits. In the ancient world, the people you ate and drank with were your friends, and your friends were the people you ate and drank with. Throughout the gospels, Jesus is referred to "a glutton and a drunkard, a friend of tax collectors and sinners" (Matt. 11:19; Luke 7:34). In the eyes of his contemporary religious authorities, Jesus was simply eating and drinking with the wrong kinds of people. They were "unclean"; he should have no association with them. We should be very eager to do the same at our own tables.

However, if the Eucharist were just about eating, we would all swarm the altar, grab what we need, and go back to our seats. That's not what happens. Just as Jesus feeds us, we feed others. We receive the cup from someone else; we receive the bread from someone else. Food is not only eaten, but shared.

Shared Hope

Whenever we share a meal with others, we repeat the generosity of a Eucharistic meal. Here is one parish's experience of Eucharistic generosity:

> Over the span of the last three decades, a wide swath of people from a city parish shared weekly meals at local homeless shelters. One year, the weekly meal fell on Christmas Day, the Feast of the Nativity. People from the parish arrived—the children a bit reluctantly because of the change from their usual Christmas Day rituals at home. Everyone shared a meal worthy of the best of Christmas Day feasts. They shared bread and wine. At the tables around the room, each person—body and soul—was present and hungry, eager for the stuff of life that nourishes. It was a reenactment of the evening before at the parish's table of the Lord. The body of Christ, broken for you. The blood of Christ, shed for you. In the myriad faces around the tables, God was present. People ate and drank together. God was host and God's people were fed.

In less dramatic ways, too, eating far away from an altar can remind Christians of the primary source of their spiritual nourishment, Holy Communion. The life of faith is less a disembodied spirituality than it is a jaw-chomping, dish-passing, wine-sipping, table-setting feast of embodiment. Our bodies are dependent on food. Our spirits are nourished by eating together with others as host or guest.

4

Singing and Worshiping

Karl was a dying man. Approaching eighty-five, his body showed pronounced signs of Parkinson's disease. He lost his ability to walk, then to speak. His mind, still active and sharp, was trapped in a body that could give expression to his thoughts only by intense effort. A pastor visited him several times, bringing him Communion that had to be served to Karl in tiny portions—just the slightest crumble of wafer and a dribble of wine. His face was blank in its affect, because the dozens of muscles required for a smile or frown were unresponsive.

A youth group visited Karl on a day in December. The youth sang two or three familiar carols and then began their finale. They were shocked as—no sooner had they sung the first words—Karl joined in singing "Silent Night." His voice was full-throated, down low, and loud! It shone through as he sang all three verses from memory with the group. It was as though he was "back," if only for a moment. And he was back because of the powerful re-membering that takes place in song.

• • •

The human body may be described as a kind of tuning fork, capable of resonance with whatever "music" surrounds and fills it. "Tune my heart to sing thy praise," we sing to God in one classic hymn.[1] The monks who chant the daily office do so, in part, to put themselves in rhythm with the music of the spheres—the sense of the rhythms of the whole universe. Spring, summer, fall, winter. Advent, Christmas, Epiphany, Lent. Allegro, adagio, scherzo, rondo.

Across time and space, human cultures join their voices with the song of creation. No one sings solo, for so many of God's creatures sing out. God waits for the creation to press play, for the curtain to rise, for the song to start. All creation tries to sing a song of praise to its Maker. Consider these words from Psalm 148:

Praise [the Lord], sun and moon;
praise him, all you shining stars!

. . . .

Praise the Lord from the earth,
. . . .
fire and hail, snow and frost,
stormy wind . . . !

Mountains and all hills,
fruit trees and all cedars!
Wild animals and all cattle,
creeping things and flying birds!

---

1. "Come Thou Fount of Every Blessing." Text: Robert Robinson, 1735–1790, alt.

. . . .

Let them praise the name of the Lord,
for his name alone is exalted. (vv. 3, 7-10, 13)

We might be tempted to think it is just an exaggeration, some kind of poetic license when the psalmist speaks about the universe singing and praising God. But a drumbeat of intermittent, regular energy pulses earthward from quasars ten billion light-years away. In a remarkable rhythm, there is in fact a kind of music of the galaxies.

In a chapter titled "The Music of *This* Sphere," biologist Lewis Thomas writes that even lowly termites "make percussive sounds to each other by beating their heads against the floor in the dark, resonating corridors of their nests."[2] Bats make sounds to use their sense of sonar, navigating among all the objects around them. But they have also been heard to produce strange, solitary, and lovely bell-like notes while hanging at rest upside down in the depths of the woods. Fish, says Thomas, "make sounds by clicking their teeth, blowing air, and drumming with special muscles against their tuned inflated air bladders." Tuned bladders! Animals with loose skeletons rattle them. Even leeches tap rhythmically on leaves. It is widely known that humpback whales sing, because recordings have been made of their songs, and we rational humans have concluded that their long, complex,

2. Lewis Thomas, *The Lives of a Cell: Notes of a Biology Watcher* (New York: Viking, 1974), 20–25.

insistent melodies are simply practical statements about navigation, or sources of food, or limits of territory. But how strange it seems, notes Thomas, that they should send "through several hundred miles of the undersea such ordinary information as 'whale here.'" Sometimes, "in the intervals between songs," they have been seen to breach and to leap clear of the waves, "landing on their backs, awash in the turbulence of their beating flippers." It is as if they were rejoicing and maybe even offering their praise for the joy of life.

All creation praises its creator. We hear only a few of the sounds at one time, but what if we could hear the combined sound that rises from the universe? Wouldn't it lift us off our feet? How could we keep from singing?

Why This Matters

Singing and worshiping do something very important for our identities. They help us balance two things that are absolutely critical for a thriving human life. Those two things are *individuation* and *participation*. Individuation means that I am me; I am *this individual* and not someone else. Participation means that I am not just me. I am also some part of a group—or many different groups. If we ignore the first, we simply float freely, coopted by forces external to us, adrift in a bland and shapeless sea. If we ignore the second, we are isolated, atomized little selves with no connection to anyone else. We have to have both.

Think about how singing with other people helps us strike the balance between the two. In singing, I assert myself with my own voice. I sing my part. I sing when it is my turn. But I also have to listen. In fact, in singing with others, I have to listen more than I sing. And this is uniquely present when people sing *together*. Churches remain the primary place in our culture where singing together is in fact the norm.

Singing in church, together, is remarkably different from other ways music is made. Karaoke is a popular pastime today, but one doesn't need to *listen* to others when singing a solo into a microphone. Hitting a pitch is less important than virtuoso trills and sloppy scoops. Singing in the shower or in the car doesn't usually involve blending your voice with the voice of another. It's wonderful to sing this way, because singing is, simply by itself, a joy. But something is missing.

One good measure of strength and togetherness in a community is how well its members sing together. In a congregation and in a choir, different voices alternate between singing loudly and softly in relationship to other voices. Each individual has to find his or her voice. Silence and listening are not ends in themselves; they are the conditions for the incubation of a voice and the production of harmony.

Singing is one of the relatively few practices that require expression of both right and left brain. It is an inherently integrative activity. It draws on our intellectual ability to read notes and text, to make sense of the flow, the rhythm, the beat. At the same time, it draws on our ability to sense and understand the emotions and feelings that are being expressed. Often singing a great hymn gives believers opportunities to discover and to express their own faith.

Shared Witness

Singing each other's music together is an act of both collaboration and discovery. The churches of the Reformation created a tradition of hymn writing and helped develop the skill of congregational singing. When the liturgical renewal movement took place in the mid-twentieth century, hundreds of Protestant and Lutheran hymns made their way into Roman Catholic worship. Singing during the worship service itself began to be a much more important part of Roman Catholic congregational life. The "work" of singing was no longer wholly delegated to a representative few, like a choir or cantor, but rather shared by the whole people gathered. Besides the songs congregations themselves sing, there are also innumerable pieces of great Christian choral music within both the Roman Catholic and Lutheran traditions. To the extent that singing remains a central part of Lutheran and Catholic worship, we can note how much we share in common in our worship and liturgical life.

As violent as the rupture was five hundred years ago, Lutherans and Roman Catholics have continued to share a liturgical tradition. Each church has continued to use a lectionary of readings from Scripture mapped onto the seasons of the church year. Following Vatican II, together we adopted a fresh and much more inclusive set of readings from the Bible (the three-year pattern of the *Revised Common*

Lectionary and the *Lectionary for Mass*). Further, both Roman Catholics and Lutherans have had to remember and appropriate a diverse tradition of Eucharistic prayers and make them available for worship, often chanting all or parts of them. In particular, each tradition in its own way has had to look at Eucharistic language and make it consistent with language expressing the priority of God's gracious creation and saving work in Jesus Christ. Both Roman Catholics and Lutherans have retrieved the beautiful prayer of the Psalter in the Liturgy of the Word, often in sung form.

When Roman Catholics began to worship in the vernacular, only a few Latin hymns had been available for regular singing. As a consequence, Roman Catholic worship leaders borrowed heavily from Lutheran and other well-developed hymnic traditions. Moreover, the gift-giving has gone both ways: since Vatican II, the Roman Catholic Church has been blessed with a number of excellent composers, who have written fresh music and new texts that are now used for worship in other Christian churches. In singing each other's songs, we come to know one another and to experience God in fresh ways.

Shared Practices

Why are the practices of singing and worshiping important as Catholics and Lutherans mark a milestone in their shared history and common faith? Singing and worshiping help us remember and they embody the senses, interrupt the usual patterns, unify peoples, and overcome division.

Remembering

Not many of us can recite an essay from memory, no matter how well written. Poems are easier to remember, but music is remembered most easily. Music helps us remember the actual words of a song. The words of a songwriter can also help call to mind and articulate a raw human emotion or story. English hymn writers Charles Wesley (1707–1788) and Isaac Watts (1674–1748) were geniuses whose insight is transmitted to us in song. People didn't used to think, "Joy to the world, the Lord is come!" but now that song easily pops into our heads with the slightest reminder.

The memory aid of singing helps individuals ("How'd that song go again?") and the community as well. Singing enables us to remember and pass along the greatest and most beautiful thoughts of human history and Christian faith. You might not know how to put into words the loss you feel at a loved one's death, but when you sing "In the Garden" or "How Great Thou Art" at a funeral, the faith of the church takes shape in your voice. The African American experience is movingly expressed in "Lift Every Voice and Sing." The first stanza ends with these lines:

> Sing a song full of the faith that the dark past has taught us;
>
> sing a song full of the hope that the present has brought us;
>
> facing the rising sun of the new day begun,
>
> let us march on till victory is won.[3]

---

3. "Lift Every Voice and Sing." Text: James W. Johnson, 1871–1938.

Such lyrics help an entire nation remember the work that lies ahead as it struggles to come to grips with legacies of slavery.

Embodying All the Senses

We tend to think of singing as being confined to the vocal folds and lungs. However, singing well is extremely sensitive to good posture, to overall bodily strength and well-being, and to the tension that one is carrying in one's shoulders, face, and other muscles. Singing requires a person to breathe well and to control the release of air through the vocal folds. Reading notes in musical phrases, rather than as individual notes, is essential for communicating musical "sense." The embodiment of singing reinforces the physicality of worship. As we worship, we stand, sit, kneel, sing, smell, taste, see, listen, touch, speak, and walk. And worship in each of our traditions has a sense of liturgy, of ritual, and of stable texts from week to week, year to year.

Unifying

When we come together with a community for worship, we may still be sleepy, daydreaming, or thinking of unfinished work. Singing a hymn together in community gathers us and unites us for the task of listening to the Scriptures, unpacking them, and interpreting them for our time. The music that is chosen for a particular worship service resonates with the emotion and major themes of the day and season, and draws us into harmony with them. As theologian Bernard Lonergan notes, emotions are the "mass and momentum of conscious living. Without our emotions, our thinking, understanding, willing, and deciding would be paper thin."[4] Singing draws our emotions to the surface, where they can be touched and transformed. Singing makes our tuning fork hum with the rhythm of the Christian life, the liturgical year, and the community around us.

Lutheran theologian Dietrich Bonhoeffer was tasked with developing a seminary to serve the Confessing Church in Germany in the 1930s. The Confessing Church expressly objected to Hitler and his policies. Hitler had been able to co-opt great portions of both the Lutheran and Roman Catholic churches in Germany, effectively causing them to forget their centuries-long commitment to justice and peace. Reflecting on his experience in that community, Bonhoeffer saw how singing brought unity to the seminarians in their resistance to a wicked ideology:

> It is the voice of the church that is heard in singing together. It is not I who sing, but the church. However, as a member of the church, I may share in its song. Thus, all true singing together must serve to widen our spiritual horizon. It must enable us to recognize our small community as a member of the great Christian church on earth and must help us willingly and joyfully to take our place in the song of the church with our singing, be it feeble or good.[5]

4. Bernard Lonergan, *Method in Theology* (Toronto: University of Toronto Press, 1973), 30–31.
5. Dietrich Bonhoeffer, *Life Together* and *Prayerbook of the Bible*, Dietrich Bonhoeffer Works, vol. 5, trans. Daniel W. Bloesch and James H. Burtness (Minneapolis: Fortress Press, 2005), 68.

Overcoming Divisions

During the great upheaval in South Africa at the end of the twentieth century, one of the most important moves toward reconciliation was to teach different racial groups the songs of "the other" and sing them together. To sing a song of the other, to respect others' music as an expression of their culture and lives, to move with them in bringing it to life, creates respect.

One of the ways Roman Catholic communities observe the Church Unity Octave (the third week of January) is to bring together people from a number of Christian congregations for a hymn sing, selecting hymns that are part of the musical heritage of each of the communities present. Most people are not explicitly aware of the origin of the hymns that are sung in their worship, so the focus naturally turns to what is held in common.

Interrupting

Imagine a bustling cafeteria. Conversations are happening at every table. People can barely hear one another. Then a group arrives and begins to sing grace. Almost by instinct, conversations quiet down and silence is granted for the interrupting singers. The national anthem sung at a game or a group of carolers breaking into Christmas song has the same effect. Singing interrupts our rhythms with its own rhythm, calling us to attention.

A more chilling example of the in-breaking quality of singing is shared by scholar and musician Don Saliers. During the violent unrest in El Salvador in the 1980s, a mass rape and murder terrorized the town of El Mozote. One of the youngest victims, Saliers writes, "did not weep or scream as she was assaulted. Instead she sang hymns. . . . The soldiers were stupefied; then they wondered and grew afraid."[6] Sometimes music simply blends in to the noise around us. But at crucial moments, the sung word cuts through and shocks, jarring us to notice what we otherwise would miss.

Shared Hope

Singing is a skill and a practice that one can cultivate. In that sense, the singer is in charge of it. But singing is also a gift that comes from God, and to that extent, the singer does not control the singing. Lots of things are like that—gift and task. God's commandments are both. A life lived according to the gospel is both. Cultivating the practice of singing, both as a gift and as a task, will help us grow together as Christians, making music together all the while.

Ecumenical work between Lutherans and Roman Catholics has been described as a "mutual exchange of gifts."[7] In few places has this exchange led to such an abundance of riches for both churches as in their singing traditions. For many who are happy to leave the finer points of doctrine to

6. Don Saliers, "Singing Our Lives," in *Practicing Our Faith: A Way of Life for a Searching People*, 2nd ed., ed. Dorothy C. Bass (San Francisco: Jossey-Bass, 2010), 189.

7. Margaret O'Gara, *The Ecumenical Gift Exchange* (Collegeville, MN: Liturgical Press, 1998); Risto Saarinen, *God and the Gift: An Ecumenical Theology of Giving*, Unitas (Collegeville, MN: Liturgical Press, 2005). See also Second Vatican Council, Dogmatic Constitution on the Church (*Lumen Gentium*), November 21, 1964, par. 13, in *Vatican Council II: The Conciliar and Postconciliar Documents*, ed. Austin Flannery, new revised edition (Collegeville, MN: Liturgical Press, 2014).

specialists, singing each other's music is the flesh and blood of greater church unity. In other words, singing and worship have been a fertile area of applied ecumenism where the body of Christ is re-membered. Singing does not just feel good, it *does* good. One adjective often given for the hopes of our churches is that their unity will be more *visible*. Singing will bring our families and our churches closer together in an *audible* unity, too.

5

Forgiving and Reconciling

After Apartheid ended in South Africa, a white police officer named Mr. Van der Broek was put on trial. The court found that he had come to a woman's home, shot her son at point-blank range, and then burned the young man's body on a fire while he and his officers partied nearby. The woman's husband was killed by the same men, and his body also was burned.

The woman was present in the courtroom and heard the confessions offered by Mr. Van der Broek. At one point, a member of South Africa's Truth and Reconciliation Commission turned to her and asked, "So, what do you want? How should justice be done for this man?"

"I want three things," the woman said confidently. "I want first to be taken to the place where my husband's body was burned so that I can gather up the dust and give his remains a decent burial."

She continued, "My husband and son were my only family. I want, secondly, for Mr. Van der Broek to become my son. I would like for him to come twice a month to the ghetto and spend a day with me so that I can pour out on him whatever love I still have.

"And, finally, I would like Mr. Van der Broek to know that I offer him my forgiveness because Jesus Christ died to forgive. This was also the wish of my husband. And so, I would kindly ask someone to come to my side and lead me across the courtroom so that I can take Mr. Van der Broek in my arms, embrace him, and let him know that he is truly forgiven."[1]

• • •

Human beings and human institutions invariably hurt each other. Pain and harm are inevitable. But forgiveness and reconciliation are not. They must happen intentionally, carefully, and habitually. They rarely, if ever, just happen. For this reason, forgiving is something we must practice. As children, a brother and sister may love one another, but of course sometimes they end up hurting each other. When that happens, their mother says, "Now apologize to your sister." "I'm sorry." "Okay, now forgive your brother." "All right, I forgive you." This is a habit we have to be helped into, a practice to be cultivated. The South African woman who lost her husband and son chose forgiveness over a legitimate demand for justice. She chose to forgive "because Jesus Christ died to forgive."

---

1. Michael Wakely, *Can It Be True? A Personal Pilgrimage through Faith and Doubt* (Grand Rapids: Kregel, 2004), 207–8.

Here is a working definition of such forgiveness: *to renounce anger or resentment against someone.* It is the act of overcoming and letting go of the anger and hatred directed toward another person or another institution as a result of harm done. When we are able to do that, we can speak of forgiving. In that sense, we speak of "granting pardon" to another—that is, not holding back against the other. This is a first step toward reconciliation.

Why This Matters

It is a tragedy that for many people, *punishment* has become a synonym for *justice.* The story of the South African woman is a miracle, because no one could deny that punishment would be just in that dreadful case. Retribution has its place, within appropriate limits. Yet there are many situations where no amount of punishment would make right the harms that have been done. And to equate justice with punishment, with no place for reconciliation and forgiveness, ignores the gospel. Forgetting forgiveness in our daily lives is a recipe for bitterness, a sure way to perpetuate a cycle of pain.

Some are reluctant to forgive because they worry that forgiving means forgetting. It might seem that over time, an injury will fade from memory without a conscious effort on our part. Forgiveness, however, is a *conscious choice* we make to let go of the anger and resentment we feel—not solely for the sake of the wrongdoer, but also for our own good and for the good of all. Similarly, the members of an institution cannot simply forget the harm done to them by the members of another institution by pretending that it did not occur. Even in the moments when we least expect it, resentment or anger can bubble to the surface as a stray comment or an act of reprisal.

The decision to forgive, to let go of resentment, does not happen immediately. The apostle Paul urges us to forgive before the sun goes down (Eph. 4:26), but it almost always takes much more time than that. Individuals as well as institutions—even churches—need to realize their need to forgive. They also need time to accept the forgiveness of another. The Lutheran–Roman Catholic dialogue has shown that in the case of institutions, as with individuals, full reconciliation is a journey, an often narrow and winding path. It is easy to lose our way, to get sidetracked, or to take a wrong turn.

Shared Witness

Catholics and Lutherans have come together theologically in many ways, but perhaps in none more important than our understanding of forgiveness and reconciliation. In that sense, these practices are not restricted to individuals. Consider the following ways that Lutheran and Roman Catholic institutions have sought ways to forgive and reconcile.

In 1963, during Vatican II, Pope Paul VI addressed the invited delegation of observers and guests from other Christian churches: "Our heart beats faster both because of the inexpressible consolation and reasonable hope that [your] presence stirs up within us, as well as because of the deep sadness we feel at [our] prolonged separation." Paul VI continued, "If we are in any way to blame for the separation, we humbly beg God's forgiveness and ask pardon too of our brethren who feel themselves to have been injured by us."[2]

We have come to realize, after fifty years of ecumenical efforts, that it was much easier to break the body of Christ than it is to put it back together. Much remains to be done, over many years and at all levels of our respective churches, to create a culture of forgiveness and reconciliation that reaches into our families and communities. Forgiveness is a process that occurs within individuals, in communities, and between institutions. And it is different from repentance, restitution, and reconciliation. Too often we confuse these with forgiveness.

The first step toward forgiveness takes us back to the opening chapter of this book, which described the task of remembering, recalling, and re-membering. In the case of re-membering the body of Christ, forgiveness requires balanced, painstaking historical research to understand better what actually happened during and after the Reformation in such a way that overstatement, hyperbole, and resentment are removed from our memories. We must recognize that we all stand knee-deep in history; there is no neutral place to stand when making judgments about the past. Such interpretation has to be done by Lutherans and Catholics together to create a common memory and to come to the best account of the

2. Address by Pope Paul VI at the opening of the second session, September 29, 1963, *AAS*, LV, 1963, pp. 841–59, here p. 853. English translation available in *Council Daybook*, Sessions 1 and 2, p. 148.

past and the moral accountability of all involved for what occurred.

Anticipating the arrival of the new millennium, Pope John Paul II succinctly expressed the need for Christians to repent and seek forgiveness:

> Among the sins which require a greater commitment to repentance and conversion should certainly be counted those which have been detrimental to the unity willed by God for his People. In the course of the thousand years now drawing to a close, even more than in the first millennium, ecclesial communion has been painfully wounded, a fact for which, at times, men of both sides were to blame. Such wounds openly contradict the will of Christ and are a cause of scandal to the world. These sins of the past unfortunately still burden us and remain ever present temptations. It is necessary to make amends for them, and earnestly to beseech Christ's forgiveness.[3]

The hard, persistent work toward forgiveness and reconciliation is never finished, not between individuals, and not between Roman Catholics and Lutherans in their ecumenical efforts.

However, there are tangible fruits along the way, always the graced work of the Holy Spirit. For example, in preparation for the commemoration of 2017, the Lutheran–Roman Catholic Commission on Unity produced *From Conflict to Communion.*[4] This resource recognizes the need for forgiveness and reconciliation: "As the

---

3. Saint John Paul II, *Apostolic Letter on Preparation for the Jubilee of the Year 2000* (*Tertio Millennio Adveniente*), November 10, 1994.

4. Lutheran–Roman Catholic Commission on Unity, *From Conflict to Communion* (Leipzig: Evangelische Verlangsanstalt / Bonifatius, 2013).

commemoration in 2017 brings joy and gratitude to expression, so must it also allow room for both Lutherans and Catholics to experience the pain over failures and trespasses, guilt and sin in the persons and events that are being remembered."[5] Lutherans on the commission were explicit about the mistakes of the past, including especially vicious and degrading statements made by adherents to Lutheran thought and tradition. And even though they agree in part with Luther's criticism of the papacy, Lutherans reject his identification of the pope with the Antichrist.[6]

Together, Roman Catholics and Lutherans acknowledged the prejudices, misunderstandings, and false characterizations of one another that occurred during our five hundred years apart.[7] Clearly, a long institutional history of reconciliation between Roman Catholic and Lutheran churches is taking place. Apart from that, both churches can learn from each other about the ordinary practices of forgiveness and reconciliation in daily life.

Shared Practices

Our minds store memories in categories. We create narratives and understandings for ourselves by linking certain thoughts and memories with similar ones, and we store them together in certain mental boxes. We have the "life is unfair" box and the "this is what she's like" box. When we have been hurt or betrayed, we often create a grievance story for ourselves,

5. Ibid., 228.
6. Ibid., 229.
7. Ibid., 233.

and this is stored in a box of grievance stories. When we are feeling sad and hurt, when we are wounded, our mind and memory go to one of these boxes and begin to make sausage, stringing all of these awful things together in a narrative. If our pain is caused by a particular person, we begin to bring together a set of grievances (all the ways that this person has treated us badly) in a narrative. We can begin to rehearse this narrative, adding, enhancing, and refining it. Of course, every time we do this exercise, we find ourselves angry or depressed, sad and powerless. The narrative can become an obsession, not readily allowing space for other more life-giving and healthy thoughts and feelings.[8] The creation of such stories happens not only on the level of persons, but also on that of communities, institutions, and nations.

Remaining stuck within this narrative brings us a kind of spiritual death. The symptoms of this death are bitterness, relentless criticism (not just of the one at fault, but everybody), sarcasm, cynicism, and intolerance. Everyone knows people who have not moved beyond their resentment and who live lives of unhappy isolation. Anger and resentment are obsessive emotions. They give the person who has done me harm rent-free space in my head.

How does one get this narrative out of one's head? Think of the mind as a television with many channels. From this point of view, not forgiving leaves the remote control stuck on the grievance channel, so it plays endless episodes of *I Had*

8. This section on creating a grievance story draws heavily on the work of Fred Luskin, *Forgive for Good: A Proven Prescription for Health and Happiness* (San Francisco: Harper, 2002).

Lousy Parents; *My Life Has Been Unfair*; *She Got the Elevator, I Got the Shaft*; or *Terrible Bosses*. Metaphorically, to get out of this situation, we need to change the channel to stations that will heal us and build us up, through the work of the Holy Spirit.

Gratitude

When we feel stuck in our grievances, it is important to remember that there is a gratitude channel, too. Members of Alcoholics Anonymous speak of living out of gratitude—for sobriety, for one's life, and for the gifts of intelligence, capacity for feeling, and honesty and integrity. When we step into the shower each morning, we can say a prayer of thanks for hot running water that billions of humans on this planet do not have. We can be grateful for the communities and places that are so much a part of our lives. We can give thanks for our religious communities and the rich, if imperfect, traditions out of which we live.

There is also a beauty channel with its countless programs: the beauty of the natural world, the colors of birds and squirrels, the way things hold and work together in nature, the way that words sound as they are spoken, and the emotional expressiveness of music. There is also a channel that features the sheer humor of the human condition. There are love and forgiveness channels, too. We can replace the grievance narrative of pain, anger, and resentment—change the channel!—with any of these others.

Letting Go of Anger

The most harmful memory channels or categories of memories are those that remind us of times when we have been helpless or angry. Memories of painful events decrease our self-confidence, our confidence in other people, and our confidence in God. When these memories have control of our minds, they create a devastating situation—one we can hardly get through without friends. This is where the support of community members or family can save us from ourselves. But that means we have to let others in and be vulnerable enough to talk about this dark place. We have to trust others to love us, to let them teach us to never despair of the mercy of God. We have to give others permission to break up our pity party and help us change the channel. It is then that the Holy Spirit can work in us, leading us to healing.

Letting go of anger is the doorway to forgiving, but can I forgive my friend's brother who raped her when she was a child? Can we forgive the perpetrators of gross violations of justice and horrific crimes against humanity? Can we forgive those who have abused the people for whom they were supposed to care? It seems that only the ones to whom the injury was done can actually grant forgiveness; it is not ours to give. But in some cases, we are, in effect, "secondary victims." Listening to a friend's pain, we may feel outrage. We need to attend to these powerful experiences of anger and helplessness too, or risk being stuck in spiritual death.[9]

---

9. See Dennis Linn, Sheila Fabricant Linn, and Matthew Linn, *Don't Forgive Too Soon: Extending the Two Hands That Heal* (Mahwah, NJ: Paulist, 1997).

Forgiveness

Forgiveness involves making some very important distinctions. It does not mean saying that what was done to us was okay, condoning injustice, accepting someone's destructive behavior, or excusing that person from responsibility. In fact, to forgive is always in some sense to place blame, to recognize that a serious wrong has been done—but I, the injured, refuse to be overcome by it. The following helpful shorthand helps to distinguish these elements:[10]

Forgiveness + Repentance = Reconciliation

Both persons—the one who was injured and the one who did the injury—need to consciously experience the essential elements of forgiveness and repentance. Only then is the possibility of reconciliation real.

Forgiveness can be offered unilaterally. We can forgive those who don't know they have hurt us, just as Christ did on the cross, forgiving those who "do not know what they are doing" (Luke 23:34). We can forgive someone even when the person may not know of it. We can forgive someone who is dead and unable to receive our forgiveness. In situations like these, forgiveness releases us from the corrosive burden of anger or bitterness that may eat away at our hearts and deaden our spirits. It opens us to the possibilities of peace and renewal. When we can finally let go of the resentment

---

10. Ibid.

and weight of an unforgiving heart, we are once again in harmony with the world around us. We are once again in tune with and participating in God's intention for the world.

Repentance

Repentance is not remorse. With remorse, there is often no willingness to change, just a continual "I'm sorry." Being sorry isn't enough. A change of behavior is necessary. True repentance is a decision followed by action, a turning around. I need to resolve not to injure again. For most of us, that can become a sincere and continuous movement toward self-knowledge and conversion, especially with help from a spiritual guide.

Repentance needs a form of restitution. Sometimes restitution is an apology to the person we have offended. Sometimes it takes the form of efforts toward new behavior. Sometimes it is money restored, legal fees paid, or even a prison term served. It may entail community service or working against injustice. All of these are actions toward restoring the peace that was violated, the unity that was broken, and the dignity and integrity of persons whose lives were shattered.

The same dynamic holds true for institutions. Institutions can commit to changing their fundamental ways of relating to others. This is what happened fifty years ago between the Lutheran and Roman Catholic churches. We have encouraged prayer in common. We now recognize each other's baptisms as valid. There are no redos, no conditional rebaptizing. We provide pastoral care and welcome to Lutheran–Catholic married couples. We have worked toward agreement on a common lectionary of Scripture readings and on the translation of key shared texts. We realize that any commemoration of the Reformation requires forgiveness and reconciliation for the sins of the past.

Shared Hope

One hot summer Sunday afternoon, after celebrating Mass with his parish community, a Catholic priest received a call from his brother Ken, whose Lutheran spouse, Shirley, was in the hospital. Ken and Shirley had just learned that she was terminally ill with stomach cancer. Would the priest come and offer her the sacrament of anointing? "Yes, of course, right away," he responded. Although Ken and Shirley were not churchgoing people, they both wanted the sacrament at this time.

The family gathered and listened together to the Scriptures, prayed for Shirley, performed the laying on of hands, and anointed her with holy oil. It was powerful, pastoral, and exactly the right thing to do. It was a moment of healing and holiness for the entire family, made possible through the work of forgiveness and reconciliation that has occurred between Lutherans and Roman Catholics during the past fifty years, re-membering the body of Christ.

6

Serving and Seeking Justice

About six miles outside the city limits of Tegucigalpa, the capital of Honduras, the municipal garbage dump sits atop acres of mountainous land, surrounded by settlements built from scraps of old wood, tin, or tires. Thousands of adults and children survive each day by scavenging off the refuse of the city.

One day a team on a weeklong service trip built a house for a family of five living in one of the settlements near the dump. Men and boys from the local community joined in the work of carrying lumber and digging holes. When the sixteen-by-sixteen-foot wooden structure was finished, members of the team gathered with the family and other members of the community to give thanks and ask God's blessing on the new home.

Team members were moved to tears by the sound of many voices praying, "Gracias, gracias, Señor" (Thank you, Lord) with a fervor not often heard in North American churches. In this bleak place, a home—however simple—was cause for gratitude. Smiles and snippets of conversation with the people reminded team members of our common humanity, the presence of God in every person, although this recognition deepened a sense of outrage that any of God's children should live in such conditions.

· · ·

Firsthand experience of such intense suffering makes us ache. We feel diminished by what we see, and we understand with new insight what the apostle Paul wrote to the Corinthians: "If one part suffers, all the parts suffer with it" (1 Cor. 12:26). We may joke with someone, "I feel your pain." But sometimes we laugh to keep from crying. As humans, we're hardwired for *compassion*; we literally "feel with" each other.

What would it take to meet the basic needs of all the world's people and for them to live with dignity and peace? The experience of meeting people through face-to-face service brings little satisfaction if we know the legacies of colonialism, exploitation, and corruption that are part of the history of Central America and other places in the world. In this context, service deepens our discomfort with the privileged place we occupy in the world. Though we may change a few habits in order to support more just economic systems, it is a struggle to know what to do to make a meaningful difference.

Why This Matters

Faith made active in loving service to the world is a deep and abiding element of Christian life. Active concern for the needs of the poor and the least in the eyes of society—or simply those needing a helping hand on a particular day—is a fundamental part of the tradition. It is a basic response to the gospel invitation to love one's neighbor as oneself. Yet there is also a danger in emphasizing "service" alone as a Christian practice because this can easily become a mask for paternalism and inequality, not to mention the danger of finding prideful satisfaction in one's own acts. The mind-set of "us" helping "them" not only is potentially disempowering for "them" but also reinforces the social divisions that plague our world.

The practice of service, therefore, must be coupled with the pursuit of justice—that is, ensuring that each person is given his or her "due" as a child of God. Loving service addresses particular needs and awakens hearts to the larger need for justice in the world. Alongside of that, the commitment to justice addresses the forces that cause such dramatic inequity in the availability of resources.

The task of seeking justice is challenging for many reasons. Christian faith that goes beyond acts of service to seeking justice in the world can be controversial. In part, this is because questions of justice confront us with the complexity and scale of our social, economic, and political systems. In addition, questions of justice force us to examine our own positions of comfort and privilege. And so faith itself is a necessary foundation for Christian justice-seeking, whether within our own homes and neighborhoods or at a national or international level.

Shared Witness

Historically, the question of the relationship of good works to faith was the major doctrinal issue dividing Lutherans and Catholics. However, through a commitment to dialogue, it has also been one of the areas of greatest success in overcoming past disagreements. The *Joint Declaration on the Doctrine of Justification* offers a "differentiated consensus" between these two traditions. In it, both traditions affirm that it is "by grace alone, in faith that Christ's saving work and not by any merit on our part" that "we are accepted by God and receive the Holy Spirit, who renews our hearts while equipping and calling us to good works."[1] At the same time, as the Lutheran-Catholic report *From Conflict to Communion* guiding the common commemoration of 2017 says, "Both Lutherans and Catholics can recognize the value of good works in view of a deepening of the communion with Christ."[2]

Indeed, it may be precisely through the different emphases of service and justice-seeking that Catholics and Lutherans can live more fully into the promise of the *Joint Declaration*. While our approaches to morality and social ethics diverged sharply in the past, today these differences of emphasis are

---

1. Lutheran World Federation and Roman Catholic Church, *Joint Declaration on the Doctrine of Justification* (Grand Rapids, MI: Eerdmans, 2000), par. 15.
2. Lutheran–Roman Catholic Commission on Unity, *From Conflict to Communion* (Leipzig: Evangelische Verlangsanstalt / Bonifatius, 2013), 133.

more likely to be complementary than antagonistic. Luther had a notion that God's activity in the world comes in a twofold way, in two spheres or "kingdoms"—the worldly, which is a place of conflict and coercion, and the heavenly, which is formed by spirit and grace. This distinction has sometimes been interpreted in ways that have encouraged culpable inaction in the face of grave injustice. Too often, loving service to the neighbor in need never questions *why* the neighbor is needy. The mandates of Catholic social teaching, which proclaim that personal faith and the mission of the church cannot be separated from action on behalf of justice, might be a helpful corrective. The Lutheran instinct leads to mercy for specific people, and the Catholic instinct leads to justice-seeking for all people. Each view needs the other.

The document *Justice in the World* that issued from the 1971 Roman Catholic Synod of Bishops says:

5. Listening to the cry of those who suffer violence and are oppressed by unjust systems and structures, and hearing the appeal of a world that by its perversity contradicts the plan of its Creator, we have shared our awareness of the Church's vocation to be present in the heart of the world by proclaiming the Good News to the poor, freedom to the oppressed, and joy to the afflicted. The hopes and forces which are moving the world in its very foundations are not foreign to the dynamism of the Gospel, which through the power of the Holy Spirit frees people from personal sin and from its consequences in social life. . . .

34. . . . Christian love of neighbor and justice cannot be separated. For love implies an absolute demand for justice, namely a recognition of the dignity and rights of one's

neighbor. Justice attains its inner fullness only in love. Because every person is truly a visible image of the invisible God and a sibling of Christ, the Christian finds in every person God himself and God's absolute demand for justice and love.[3]

At the same time, Luther's attention to the power and pervasiveness of sin in the world tempers a naive optimism in Lutherans and Catholics alike about the effects of our human action for justice in the world. Simultaneously and paradoxically, it offers a bold freedom to act, trusting that God's kingdom is *God's* kingdom, not ours. While the Catholic tradition's emphasis on personal virtue and the works of mercy can be a helpful guide in the moral life, Catholics do well to remember that service is an act of joy born of gratitude for the merciful love of God. Citing the Lutheran *Formula of Concord,* the *Annex to the Joint Declaration on the Doctrine of Justification* states, "The working of God's grace does not exclude human action: God effects everything, the willing and the achievement, therefore, we are called to strive (cf. Phil 2:12 ff). 'As soon as the Holy Spirit has initiated his work of regeneration and renewal in us through the Word and the holy sacraments, it is certain that we can and must cooperate by the power of the Holy Spirit.'"[4]

---

3. World Synod of Bishops, *Justice in the World* (*De Justicia in Mundo*), 1971.
4. Lutheran World Federation and Roman Catholic Church, *Annex to the Joint Declaration on the Doctrine of Justification*, 2C.

Shared Practices

So how might we faithfully and effectively live out the commitment to serving and seeking justice in the world?

Bringing a Variety of Gifts to Serving and Seeking Justice

First, it is essential to remember that every person is called and gifted in distinct ways. This is precisely why Christians are gathered into a body that is more than the sum of its parts. The team working outside Tegucigalpa relied heavily on the skills and construction expertise of a few of its members to direct progress. Others gifted with language ability were indispensable for communication with local people. Still others brought sheer physical strength, a sense of humor and encouragement, medical knowledge, or a special connection with children. These many and varied gifts were all important to the service offered by the team. Paul writes to the church in Corinth:

> There are varieties of gifts, but the same Spirit; and there are varieties of services, but the same Lord; and there are varieties of activities, but it is the same God who activates all of them in everyone. To each is given the manifestation of the Spirit for the common good. . . .
>
> For just as the body is one and has many members, and all the members of the body, though many, are one body, so it is with Christ. . . .
>
> Indeed, the body does not consist of one member but of many. If the foot would say, "Because I am not a hand, I do not belong to the body," that would not make it any less a part of the body. And if the ear would say, "Because I am not an eye, I do not belong to the body," that would not make it any less a

> part of the body. If the whole body were an eye, where would the hearing be? If the whole body were hearing, where would the sense of smell be? But as it is, God arranged the members in the body, each one of them, as he chose. If all were a single member, where would the body be? As it is, there are many members, yet one body. The eye cannot say to the hand, "I have no need of you," nor again the head to the feet, "I have no need of you." (1 Cor. 12:4-7, 12, 14-21)

Just as each member makes unique and essential contributions to our work as a whole, serving the neighbor and seeking justice are also unique and essential contributions to the work of re-membering the body of Christ in the world. It is not necessary—and can in fact be a barrier to unity—for all to serve in the same way. Rather, an approach to service that is open and attentive to ways of bringing a variety of distinct vocations into contact with the needs of the world is sustainable over time. It also witnesses beautifully to the unity and diversity of the body of Christ.

The same is true of pursuing justice at a more structural level. Not everyone has the expertise, abilities, and passions for crafting policy or engaging in civil protest. Yet this is not a reason to despair of serving the world and seeking justice. It is a reminder that we each are called to play a part and is cause for rejoicing in the diverse gifts we have to offer.

Seeking the Truth about Social Inequality and Injustice

Furthermore, we need to remain conscious about the attitudes we hold toward those we serve, resisting the condescending tendency to see them only as recipients of our merciful goodwill. In fact, we likely are privileged beneficiaries of an unjust system that perpetuates their misery. Vincent de Paul (1581–1660) makes a provocative statement about the practice of Christian charity:

> You will find out that Charity is a heavy burden to carry, heavier than the bowl of soup and the full basket. But you will keep your gentleness and your smile. It is not enough to give soup and bread. This the rich can do. You are the servant of the poor, always smiling and good-humored. They are your masters, terrible, sensitive and exacting masters, as you will soon see. The uglier and the dirtier they will be, the more unjust and insulting, the more love you must give them. It is only for your love alone, that the poor will forgive you the bread you give to them.[5]

This final sentence points to the fact that the fullness of love can bear to look the hungry or homeless neighbor in the eye only when it also examines why social inequality and injustice persist. Even as we seek to serve and build relationships at the most local levels, we also need to remain diligent in examining how the needs of our particular communities are connected to events and trends in the wider world. In an age of hashtags and tweets, when we can select the news channels that conform to our preferred ideology, a commitment to truth is more essential than ever for Christians—even and especially when that truth is complex or uncomfortable.

---

5. Megan McKenna, *Send My Roots Rain: A Spirituality of Justice and Mercy* (New York: Doubleday, 2003), 246–47.

Shared Hope

A mystery hidden in the practice of service is that servants often receive as much as or more than they give. Joy comes to them in the connections that are built, both among the ones who serve and with the ones served. Joy comes from seeing the just fruits of good service, and comfort comes from knowing that if we cannot see the fruit, at least we can plant the seeds. Others will water and tend them. Like other practices in this book, service really is a joyful human activity, even if it is not always fun. It opens our eyes, which tends to have the effect of opening our hearts and maybe even our minds, wallets, and voices.

Those who serve in the name of Jesus are blessed by a unique contribution of Christian faith: because Christians trust in God who brings justice, they need not have the end exactly in mind when beginning their service. They are free to serve in whichever way seems best at the time. Service thus gives expression to human freedom. In fact, one might go so far as to say that freedom *is* service, and service, freedom.[6] No matter whether one travels to Honduras or volunteers at the local parish, the one who serves takes an important journey into the depths of human compassion and unity.

When the American media began to report thousands of children crossing the U.S. border to flee gang-related violence in Honduras and Guatemala, Lutheran and Catholic leaders spoke for the rights of those young people. For those who have served in places like Tegucigalpa, those news

6. Martin Luther, *On Christian Liberty* (Minneapolis: Fortress Press, 2003).

reports are much more real and personal. Remembering the faces of the children, we are heartbroken that the world's injustice and violence are so tenacious. Remembering God's victory over sin and death, we are emboldened and empowered to join the struggle for justice.

We trust that, however overwhelming the problems of the world may be, God is greater. Speaking to his disciples of the injustices both he and they will suffer, Jesus explains that he has told them of these things so that they may have peace and take courage, "for I have overcome the world" (John 16:33). Furthermore, we can take comfort in the knowledge that even if our best attempts at serving and seeking justice appear to be ineffective, Jesus is merciful to us in our weak and faltering efforts and promises, "Blessed are those who hunger and thirst for righteousness, for they will be filled" (Matt. 5:6).

7

Dying and Grieving

"The patient in 206 wants a rabbi," the desk nurse told the chaplain who was on call that night.

"I'm Lutheran. Does that count?"

"I'm not sure. Better go in there."

The man was not doing well. The end of a long battle with emphysema was near, and the patient knew it. It was the middle of the night, the spiritual-care staff of the hospital had gone home, and the staff rabbi was on vacation. The on-call chaplain, an intern, explained this to the patient, who said not to trouble anyone else. The chaplain knew enough about Judaism to know the prayer the patient might want to pray, the Shema: "Hear, O Israel: the Lord is God, the Lord is one" (from Deut. 6:4). Observant Jews pray it in the morning and evening, and it is especially appropriate at death.

The chaplain went to the chapel and found a tallith, the Jewish prayer shawl with fringed tassels. He placed it in the patient's lap, and the man held one tassel between his thumb and forefinger. The two spoke together, the chaplain's voice loud and the patient's faint and growing fainter: "Shema Yisrael. Adonai eloheinu. Adonai echad." The chaplain helped the man move his fingers to the next tassel. They said the words again: "Hear, O Israel: the Lord is God, the Lord is one." The chaplain moved the man's fingers again, and again, repeating the prayer—not a prayer, necessarily, as much as a statement about who God is and therefore who we are. The patient mouthed the words as his ability to speak gradually left him. The chaplain, through his tears, finished the prayer on the last tassel. Then the patient died.

. . .

It is difficult to talk about a good death. Isn't that like a squared circle—a contradiction in terms? After all, death is God's enemy, one that God has promised in the end to defeat. This is a book about practices that remember the body, the embodiedness of life, even spiritual life. And we hope that this remembering will help re-member the body of Christ, the church, which has been dismembered by division. So it might seem strange to have a chapter on dying, because dying is not something that one can "practice" any more than a basketball player can practice being tall.

But no matter how much we would like to ignore the fact, we will all die. And whether we acknowledge it or not, the inevitability of death has a way of shaping our lives. This is a nonnegotiable element of the human condition, so we might as well think about approaches to dying and grieving that can affirm our lives and renew our loves. Lutherans and

Catholics have learned about these practices from each other. Therefore, we are bold to claim that these practices have something to say to everyone about death and grief.

Why This Matters

A recent survey asked Americans how they wanted to die. Three responses emerged: Americans wanted to die quickly; they wanted to die in their sleep, without knowing that it was coming; and they did not want to be a burden on anyone. Being surrounded by loved ones might be nice, but survey respondents did not want to cause sadness for their families.

In the long arc of human history, these hopes for death are incredibly unusual. For example, in the Great Litany of the *Book of Common Prayer*, which Anglicans pray especially during the season of Lent, when thoughts turn naturally to death and new life, Anglicans pray to be delivered "from dying suddenly and unprepared." The approach of death is seen as a final chance for reconciliation with God and with others. Dying unprepared means withholding forgiveness from those who have wronged me or robbing someone of the chance to make things right with me.

Mourning rituals in some other cultures are highly scripted and unanimously shared, giving people a shared point of view and common practices for coping with death. In Japan, for example, members of the family wash the body before cremation. It's a way of touching, honoring, and saying good-bye to the deceased person. In our culture, in contrast, euphemisms multiply endlessly so we can avoid saying, "She died." We prefer "passed away," "lost her life," "passed," "crossed over," "slipped away," or "departed."

Other examples show how dysfunctional our culture has become with regard to death. In America—where youth has always been idolized—now more than ever we distance ourselves from death. Elderly parents and grandparents, not wanting to be a burden to their families, live in care facilities until they die. Usually this is not because children are unwilling or unable to help, but because the logistics of doing so have become overly complicated in our culture. We move often and far away for work. Homes are not built for extended families. And while families still gather in each other's homes to support one other and grieve together at times of death, the body of the deceased is not present as it was in the past. Then the body was often in the parlor, and conversation and sharing took place in the "living" room.

According to Amy Plantinga Pauw in her essay "Dying Well,"[1] the two institutions that have contributed more than any others to modern sensibilities about death are the hospital and the funeral home. Both have helped to remove death from rhythms of life. The things of death happen there, rather than in one's home. These institutions are likely here to stay, so it makes sense to think more deeply about what dying and grieving might mean in our own time.

1. Amy Plantinga Pauw, "Dying Well," in *Practicing Our Faith: A Way of Life for a Searching People*, 2nd ed., ed. Dorothy C. Bass (San Francisco: Jossey-Bass, 2010), 161–75.

Shared Witness

Ash Wednesday is one occasion when Christians can reflect together on death and its meaning. We allow ourselves to be marked in ashes as a reminder of our mortality: "Remember that you are dust and to dust you shall return." Ash Wednesday opens the season of Lent, a time of year when we attend to our shortcomings in preparation for Easter. We do so not to dwell in our faults, but to deepen our commitment to living the gospel.

Commemorating the solemn liturgy of the Passion of the Lord or Good Friday provides an opportunity for Catholics and Lutherans, indeed for all Christians, to reflect together on the mystery of Jesus' death and dying. Because neither communion celebrates Eucharist on Good Friday, this service draws more attention to what Christians share than what divides them. It can be planned as an ecumenical service of prayer, preaching, readings from the Passion Narrative, and veneration of the cross.

One of the issues that divided Lutherans and Catholics in the sixteenth century concerned the finality of death as reflected in the practice of the invocation of the saints. Lutherans saw this as a misguided practice of praying to dead people, whereas Catholics understood it as an important way of maintaining a connection with the faithful who had lived and died before them. A joint Lutheran-Catholic document, *The One Mediator, the Saints and Mary*, states, "Catholics asserted the legitimacy of the invocation of the saints as an authentic ecclesiastical tradition; Lutherans opposed the practice because it obscures the sole mediatorship of Christ."[2] While the dialogue concluded that our churches are still separated by differing views on the invocation of saints, it recommended two further steps for common study. Lutheran churches acknowledge that the teachings of Vatican II on the saints do not promote beliefs or practices opposed to the gospel. The Catholic Church acknowledges that Lutherans, focusing on Christ the one Mediator, are not obliged to invoke the saints.

As Ernest Becker pointed out in his classic book *The Denial of Death*,[3] the awareness of death is an engine for human creativity. We want our lives to mean something, even if they will end in death. "Who can live and never see death?" (Ps. 89:48). "Death is just a part of life" goes a popular saying. Yet Christians do not think of death as a natural event. Death is a consequence of sin. As Paul says, "The wages of sin is death" (Rom. 6:23). Central to the Christian message of hope is the conviction that death is not final: "Where, O death, is your victory? Where, O death, is your sting?" (1 Cor. 15:55).

Shared Practices

What can we say about dying and grieving from our shared perspective? Consider a few practices that might illumine the way forward.

---

2. H. George Anderson, J. Francis Stafford, and Joseph A. Burgess, eds., *The One Mediator, the Saints, and Mary*, Lutherans and Catholics in Dialogue 8 (Minneapolis: Augsburg Fortress, 1992).
3. Ernest Becker, *The Denial of Death* (New York: Free Press, 1973).

Writing a Will

One concrete practice that Lutherans and Catholics can certainly share is to have thought about death enough to have a will. This seems an obvious recommendation, but in fact, only 40 percent of Americans die with wills. What's worse, pastors and priests, who certainly ought to have thought about death and its meanings, are no more likely than their congregants to have a will.

A last will and testament is a legal document, but it is also a moral one. What we do with our money and possessions is a value-laden enterprise. We show what we care about as much by what we do with our money as by any other choices we make. Therefore, it makes sense that people of faith would want their deeply held beliefs about God to be reflected in their decisions about material possessions. We ought to have done the hard work of identifying assets and liabilities and specifying to whom or what any remaining resources should be directed. In so doing, we witness more clearly to the care we have for our family and others.

The following is an example of a preamble to a will. Notice how it sets the context of death in the Christian symbols of baptism and eternal life.

> I, _____, of the city of
> _____, and State of _____, being of
> sound and disposing mind and memory, and being under no
> restraint, do make, declare and publish this my last Will and
> Testament.
> In thanksgiving to God for the gift of life given in baptism,
> and for the many blessings God has given me; and in

thanksgiving to God for the assurance of grace, and the gifts of faith and hope through Jesus Christ; and in thanksgiving to God for the gifts of nurture and love through the church where we have shared faith and fellowship; I now commend my loved ones to grow in this same faith, to be true to their own baptism in the sure knowledge that God will continue to provide for them in their lifetime, and to place their faith and trust in our Lord and Savior Jesus Christ, not in earthly riches. The land I own, the possessions I have, have merely been borrowed by me from God. I hope I have been a good steward. "I am the Resurrection and the Life," says the Lord. "Those who believe in me, even though they die, will live" (John 11:25-26).

I now therefore . . . [and then the particulars of the Will would follow].

The reading of a will of this kind is less a sterile legal transaction and more a chance for loved ones to remember who you were and what your estate is for. It makes life the central focus and thereby puts death appropriately at the periphery.

Planning Your Funeral

The number of people who have planned their funerals and made their loved ones aware of their wishes is even fewer than the number of people who have written their wills. A funeral serves many purposes. It honors the life of the deceased. It helps survivors remember who the deceased was and what his or her life meant. But most important, it is a chance for the gospel to be proclaimed. When funerals put more emphasis on eulogizing than proclaiming, this truth is obscured.

What is a good funeral? In *Accompany Them with Singing*,[4] liturgical theologian Thomas Long argues that four things should be present in the Christian drama we call a funeral: a holy person, a holy place, a holy script, and a holy people. The holy person is the deceased—one whom we call a saint. The dead person is the reason for gathering to worship. His or her Christian life, inaugurated in baptism and now complete in God, is marked and remembered. A holy place is one where we can sense the presence of God and where we focus attention on God. A holy script remembers God's grand story of creation, redemption, and sanctification. A holy people is the congregation who cared for the deceased and gather again to hear the promises of God concerning life and death.

If funerals reflect thoughtful preparation and attend to the ways liturgy shapes our lives and our deaths, they can be healing and celebratory—not only for the family but also for the community. Sharing the life of the deceased person needs to be done with care, balancing remembrance of him or her with proclamation of the gospel. A funeral can be a rich opportunity to speak God's love and overwhelming grace in word and song. Finding a balance of focused ritual and personal remembrance is the key.

4. Thomas G. Long, *Accompany Them with Singing: The Christian Funeral* (Louisville: Westminster John Knox, 2009).

Taking Time to Grieve

As a practice, grieving is something one actively does. Suffering is what happens to you; grieving is what you do with it. We can take ownership of our grief, channel it, and give shape to it. Grieving includes remembering, because in order to have in mind the person whose loss one grieves, one must put his or her life in its proper context. After all, memories don't come in the abstract, but in particulars: the sound of her laugh or that meal he cooked, the way she held her head just to the side or the way he walked.

We do not know how many losses we will grieve, and loss often surprises us. We expect to lose our parents, but close friends or siblings can also succumb to cancer or die from an early heart attack or a fatal accident. Parents don't expect to lose a son or daughter in a tragic manner, but it happens too often. We begin to realize just how fragile and vulnerable our lives really are. It is important to grieve these losses, because they can have a cumulative effect. Many times, individuals find themselves reacting more strongly to a loss than one would expect, because despair is often a secondary reaction to an earlier loss that was not grieved.

Supporting the Grieving

The support of a community of faith can be enormously helpful in reducing the impact of grief. The line of people who come to a parent's wake and funeral bring so many stories, so many affirmations of the father or mother's goodness—not perfection, just human goodness. These affirmations turn our sorrow into a joyful remembrance of a loved one's life. This doesn't mean that tears are banished; it means that tears are quickly followed with laughter at the memories triggered by yet another story.

Shared Hope

The New Testament speaks of the final day (Rev. 21:1-5), of the blessed feast, when there is no longer any human need to make peace with death or to figure out a good coping strategy: death is *banished*. It is not fitted into a scheme that we can't yet understand—it is *defeated*. Right now, it doesn't feel that way, so we grieve. Our grief is a fitting testament to our connection to others on this earth and to the web of human meaning that is so central to human experience.

Saint Benedict instructs his monks to "keep death daily before their eyes."[5] This caution is not intended as a morbid reminder of mortality but rather as a spiritual practice that orients all of the other decisions in one's life. This orientation is coupled with these words from the *Rule of Benedict*: "And may He bring us all together to everlasting life."[6] All of our reflections on death and grieving are leavened by the hope of ultimate transformation by the Triune God.

5. *Rule of Benedict*, 4.48.
6. Ibid., 72.12.

8

Bread for the Journey

Jesus said to his disciples, "Follow me." They did.

Their journey coursed through the Galilean countryside and then on to Jerusalem. There they witnessed Jesus' passion, death, and resurrection. On the night before he died, Jesus prayed that the disciples might all be one, so that the world might believe that the Father had sent him and loved them even as he did. In Jerusalem, they received the Spirit. From Jerusalem, they went out into the world.

The ecumenical movement continues the journey that began in Galilee. Ironically, we are a broken people on pilgrimage, divided by centuries-old disagreements. Yet we journey toward that wholeness Christ prayed for the night before he died. Pope Francis said, "We must never forget that we are pilgrims journeying alongside one another. This means that we must have sincere trust in our fellow pilgrims, putting aside all suspicion or mistrust, and turn our gaze to what we are all seeking: the radiant peace of God's face."[1]

Here's where we stand today. Over the past fifty years, Lutherans and Catholics have been at the forefront of formal and informal ecumenical dialogue that has been wonderfully graced and fruitful. On October 31, 1999, officials from the Lutheran World Federation and the Roman Catholic Church formally signed the *Joint Declaration on the Doctrine of Justification*. Ongoing dialogue continued from that groundbreaking agreement. In 2013, the Lutheran–Roman Catholic Commission on Unity produced *From Conflict to Communion* for common commemoration of the Reformation in 2017.

Here's what we hope. We wrote this resource for congregations: for reading, reflection, and discussion. We urge pastors to use this resource to build spiritual unity and contribute to the healing of historic divisions at a grassroots level.

Finally, we offer this resource to Lutherans and Catholics—indeed, to all Christians—as bread for the journey.

---

1. Pope Francis, Apostolic Exhortation on the Proclamation of the Gospel in Today's World (*Evangelii Gaudium*), November 24, 2013, par. 244.

Discussion Questions

You can use this book to read and reflect on your own, and also to spark discussion in your family, neighborhood, congregation, and community.

Here are some questions to get your discussion started. Use them to talk about your experiences or to trigger other questions.

What are *your* questions? Send them to adam@ booksprints.net.

Re-Membering

1. When have you experienced God creating something new out of broken pieces or situations?
2. What is God's role in re-membering the body of Christ in the world? What part do we play in this?

Praying and Breathing

1. How do *you* get God's attention?
2. What's the simplest prayer you utter? When do you use this prayer?
3. How do you think about or describe the act of praying?
4. Give examples of situations when prayer might mean paying attention, silence, showing compassion, or sharing enthusiasm, tears, or despair.
5. What's your practice of prayer? (Remember, it can be as simple as breathing in and breathing out with intention.)
6. What prayers do you know by heart? When do you pull them out?
7. Pray the Lord's Prayer or Our Father together. What phrases in this prayer capture your imagination right now, and why? Tell about a time when you experienced this prayer being prayed in another way or with other words.

Eating and Drinking

1. Think of the best meal you ever had. Now think of the most memorable meal you ever had. In what ways do these meals remind you of the Lord's Supper?
2. Why is it important to eat and drink every day? What would cause you to skip a meal or forget to eat?
3. Why is it important to have the Eucharist every day or

every week? What would cause you to skip the Eucharist?

4. When have you been physically hungry or thirsty? When have you been spiritually hungry or thirsty? What did you do, or where did you go?

5. How do the Lord's Supper and our daily eating and drinking connect us to the earth, to one another, and to God?

Singing and Worshiping

1. What's the playlist running through your mind right now? Do you have a certain song stuck in your head? If your life had a soundtrack, what kind of music would be included?

2. When have you been moved by a song, and why? When you're happy or sad or in love or in a space you need to get out of, what music do you turn to?

3. What's your favorite hymn or song used during worship? What does it evoke for you? How does it speak to your faith?

4. Discuss how it feels to sing a song with a large group of people in these situations: at a football or baseball game, at a difficult time for you or your community, at a time of joy and celebration, in a worship service.

5. What experience of worship has been most meaningful to you, and why?

Forgiving and Reconciling

1. How do you understand forgiveness?
2. How do you understand reconciliation?
3. Think about someone you need to forgive, or someone who needs to forgive you. What needs to happen to start the process of forgiveness?
4. For you, right now, what is unforgivable? Why?
5. For you, right now, who is unforgivable? Why?
6. You find out that you harmed someone without knowing it. What do you do? If you have been in this situation, what happened?
7. What is the most challenging part of reconciliation for you?

Serving and Seeking Justice

1. Is it easier for you to give or receive help? Why?
2. Think about a time when someone helped you. How did it feel?
3. Where have you encountered extreme poverty and injustice? What did it look and feel like? What did you do?
4. Who are the neighbors in need in your life or community? What would best serve their needs?
5. Name some people you can look to as examples of serving and seeking justice in the world.

6. What gifts do you have for serving or for seeking justice?
7. Read Matthew 25:31–46. Where do you fit in this story?

Dying and Grieving

1. How do you explain death and dying to a child? To yourself?
2. How does faith help you think about the death of others and your own death?
3. How would you prefer to die?
4. If you have an up-to-date will, how does it reflect your values and faith? If you don't have a will, what's preventing you from writing one?
5. What would you like to have happen at your wake or at your funeral? What would you choose for readings, speakers, hymns, music, or food and drink?
6. What would you like to have happen to your body after death? If you have clarified your intentions, how did you feel about doing that? If you have not clarified your intentions, what's keeping you from doing this?
7. How has your church helped people in times of dying and grieving?
8. Think about the hardest loss you've experienced and how you grieved this loss. What helped in this process—and what didn't? What has grieving this loss taught you about helping others grieve?

Bread for the Journey

1. What have you learned about yourself during this study? What have you learned about other believers?
2. What hopes do you have for the journey toward unity among Jesus' followers? How will you continue this journey?